Mark Elstob

**A Trip to Kilkenny**

From Durham by way of Whitehaven and Dublin, in the Year MDCCLXXVI

Mark Elstob

**A Trip to Kilkenny**
*From Durham by way of Whitehaven and Dublin, in the Year MDCCLXXVI*

ISBN/EAN: 9783337139889

Printed in Europe, USA, Canada, Australia, Japan

Cover: Foto ©ninafisch / pixelio.de

More available books at **www.hansebooks.com**

# A TRIP TO KILKENNY.

# A TRIP TO KILKENNY,

From *DURHAM*.

BY WAY OF

*WHITEHAVEN* AND *DUBLIN*,

IN THE YEAR MDCCLXXVI.

CONTAINING

Remarks on the situations and distances of places; ———the customs and manners of the people, interspersed with short digressions,———and some observations on the climate, productions, and curiosities of Ireland.

In a SERIES of LETTERS to a FRIEND.

---

DUBLIN:
PRINTED BY J. HILLARY,
FOR THE COMPANY OF BOOKSELLERS.
MDCCLXXIX.

# PREFACE.

*THE letters which gave birth to this little book, were principally intended to amuse a near relation: But those letters not being confined to one hand, nor even to a few hands, they in a little time became almost a public manuscript.—Some requested, and all approved of, their publication.—This was a motive power sufficient to act upon any bookish machine. I therefore set to work, reciting many passages verbatim, retaining others in their original style, leaving out such as I imagined to be trifling or trite, and weaving in other materials that were judged more useful and entertaining; and, through the whole, whale*, I have purposely preserved the primitive address, as well as the original familiarity of style: But the description relative to sculpture, architecture, and painting, are almost entirely omitted, as these may be seen in Mr. Twiss's tour in Ireland.

MARK ELSTOB.

SHOTTON,
Aug. 7, 1778.

CONTENTS.

# CONTENTS.

LETTER I. *From Durham to Whitehaven,* page 9
—— II. *Whitehaven* 26
—— III. *From Whitehaven to Skerries in Ireland.* 33
—— IV. *Skerries in Ireland* 38
—— V. *Skerries continued* 54
—— VI. *A general account of Ireland;—its divisions, subdivisions or counties, parishes, measures, coins, &c.* 61
—— VII. *From Skerries to Dublin* 71
—— VIII. *Dublin, the capital of Ireland* 76
—— IX. *Dublin continued* 89
—— X. *Dublin continued* 102
—— XI. *Kilkenny stage-coach* 107
—— XII. *Kilkenny stage-coach continued* 117
—— XIII. *Kilkenny.* 124
—— XIV. *A description of the caverns near Kilkenny* 138
—— XV. *Farther remarks and occurrences in the county of Kilkenny, Whiteboys, &c.* 148

LETTER XVI. *Miscellaneous observations——On the peculiar customs of the Irish, &c.* — — 158

——— XVII. *Wales* — — 172

# A TRIP TO KILKENNY, in 1776.

---

## LETTER I.

*From DURHAM to WHITEHAVEN.*

DEAR SIR,

YOU know it to be a regular and eftablifhed Maxim among Journalifts, to fet out with fome information of the bufinefs they went upon, or the chief defign of their travelling: I fhould have complied with the fettled form, had not prudence ftood in the way, and oppofed my intention. A little timidity would have been but a feeble obfta-
cle

cle in the way of cuſtom, could I have made an introduction of that ſort either intereſting or entertaining to you, and, in the account, included none but myſelf; but neither of theſe could be done. I will therefore paſs on, with this hint to you, that, as I had but a ſingle day's warning of my departure, I was, in every reſpect, unprepared for making ſuch remarks as ſhould be the moſt proper, and moſt eſſential matter of a journal. However you will have this agreeable conſolation—The labour of reading will be but ſmall, and the time thrown away but very little:—For I ſolemnly proteſt I will not encumber my mind long with it,—juſt model off what I can beſt remember, and what I found myſelf moſt entertained with; preſuming you, and others of the ſame congeniality, will

find

find some entertainment from the reflected view, which I shall hold out to you.

At my setting out I had not the least design of committing any thing to paper but my expences: But I was soon induced, by the variety of scenes and objects which came in my way, to step out of this narrow track. Indeed I often got too far out of it; for, by being too attentive to the different scenery around me, I sometimes forgot to note down my disbursements.

You will remember I mentioned to you, that I left Durham October the 2d, in my way to Whitehaven. You will also recollect, that I told you I had made some few remarks in the road to Whitehaven. It will now

now, perhaps, be proper to add, that the firſt memorandums I made, were the diſtances and names of places through and near which we paſſed. And, as it will, I believe, be moſt agreeable, as well as render what follows more intelligible, if I give you a previous idea of my firſt route, I ſhall therefore preſent you with the following itinerant Synopſis, where the figures ſhew the *poſt* miles in each ſtage, or from one ſtage-town to another, and thoſe places which have no figures affixed, are the intermediate places between the reſpective ſtages.

From *Durham* to *Biſhop-Auckland*  10
  St. Andrew-Auckland, on the left
  Bruſſelton Folly, on the left
  St. Helen-Auckland
  Weſt-Auckland

                              Raby

# KILKENNY.

   Raby
   Raby Castle, on the right
   Stainthorp
To *Barnardcastle* — — 15
   Bowes
To *Brough* — — 17
   Brough Hill
   Bondgate
   Appleby Castle
   Appleby
   Kirkindrof
   Kirby-Fuer
   Temple-Sowerby
   Eden-Bridge
   Countess's Pillar
   Carlton Hall, on the right
   Yeoman Bridge
To *Penrith* — — 22
   Hutton Moor
   Saddle Hill, on the right
   Hutton

| | |
|---|---:|
| To *Keswick* — — | 18 |
| Skiddaw Hill, on the right | |
| Bassenthwaite Water, on the right | |
| Lorton, on the left | |
| To *Cockermouth* — | 12 |
| To *Whitehaven* — | 14 |

Post-miles from *Durham* to *Whitehaven*, 108

---

The first night after my setting out from Durham, I slept at Barnard-castle. This town consists of little more than one principal street, which runs North and South, nearly. The houses are built chiefly of free-stone, and covered with dark-blue slate. The market-cross is remarkably large; it was built at the sole expence of the late Thomas Breakes, Esq.——Some remains

remains of the castle are yet to be seen.

Next morning (October the 3d) I set off for Brough. In passing over Stainmoor, which is a large, level, barren Moor, I found the air exceedingly cold. When I came to Brough, I asked the mistress of the White-Swan Inn—Whether she found the day any colder than yesterday: But she assured me it was rather warmer. Indeed to me the day had much the same appearance as the preceding day, only I felt the air, on the Moor, much more piercing and cold.—The Moor is very extensive, and the situation is nearly upon a level with the adjacent enclosures; from which it appears, that the excessive cold must be the effect of one, or a combination on of the three following causes. *First*, The matter of cold, which adheres to the particles of the air, and is carried about with them, not meeting with any interposition from hedges, or other fences, is not dashed off, nor diminished, but perhaps rather encreased; and, by these means, the floating particles become more dense and fixt, and consequently more cold. *Second*, The matter of cold may be greatly encreased by the exhalations from the particular quality of the soil. *Third*, The momentum of the air, &c. will be much greater than in inclosures, from its meeting with no obstacle to retard its motion.—These were the thoughts that first occurred to me on reflecting on the phænomenon, and I have given them as entire and genuine as

my

my memory could difpenfe them. If any one of more learning and knowledge of thefe matters finds out other caufes, I fhall yet retain fome hope that they will not be fuch as entirely to fuperfede thofe I have fhewn above.

A few miles from Barnardcaftle, quick hedges begin to decay; the fences changing into ftone-walls without mortar.—In this ftage much fpring corn is grown, but moftly oats. The crop, they faid, was tolerably good; but when compared with thofe in Durham, Yorkfhire, and fome other adjacent counties, I knew it was very great. The oats were about half down; thofe the people were reaping appeared to be green, but the feafon being late, I fuppofe they

they did not think it proper to delay.

Brough is pleasantly situated; the town is surrounded with trees: It has a castle. About a mile from the town, towards Appleby, is the noted Brough-hill, where the fair is held. The fair had ended a few days before, and the ground, through which the road passes, had much the appearance of a fallow field, occasioned by the great numbers of cattle being so lately upon it. The lower part, on the right of the road, is the sheep-market, and the higher part, on the left, is the place for Galloways, Kiloes, &c.

Appleby is an agreeable situation. It is decorated with stately trees; and

and the country, for some distance around it, is very woody. The greatest part of the houses are built with a copper-coloured stone, and covered with slates.—At the first appearance of the town, when I could just distinguish it through the shady woods, the primitive idea I conceived was, that the houses had reared their arched heads in order to vie with the shady trees;—and indeed it is not uncommon for Art to vie with Nature.

Between Appleby and Penrith, on the right, is a long ridge of mountains, which seem to terminate opposite on the North-side of Carlton-hall. Near the termination is a pyramidal figure of stone, called Pen-
·rith·

rith Fell, or (as they pronounce it) Pearth Fell.

Between Eden-bridge and Carlton-hall, is a monument, in the lane, called Countefs's Pillar; the pedeftal is a cylinder, and the top a fquare prifm, on each fide of which is a fun-dial. It was fet up by a lady, who had accompanied her daughter, then on her way to Italy, to that place:—It happened the young lady died abroad, nor did they ever meet more,—and this pillar was erected by the mother to commemorate the laft interview.—I have not been able to collect either the lady's name, or the place of her refidence.—In this ftage I remarked a very fingular cuftom among the farmers, that is, the fetting their corn-ftacks in the corners of the fields wherein the corn had grown

grown, when no barn nor houſe is near them,

In travelling over Hutton-moor, about ſun ſetting, I viewed a beautiful phænomenon before me. From the moor a fine vale appeared right before me, and only to be ſeen through an opening between two hills, whereof Saddle-hill is that on the right-hand. The air becoming light, the vapours deſcended ſlowly down the ſides of the adjacent hills, and in a little time ſeemed to overſpread the whole valley, apparently to the diſtance of ſeveral miles. The denſe vapours, being below my horizon, appeared as ſhips moving on the light miſt as on a ſea; and their variety of forms and motions, and tranſient

tranſient duration, made the proſpect truly picturesque and delightful.

About eight o'clock I arrived at Keſwick. Here I took up my lodgings. The town has a market on Saturday. At the diſtance of about two miles is the famous *Derwent Lake*; and a little further to the Weſt is Baſſenthwaite Lake: But I had not the opportunity of viſiting either. Much people reſort here in ſummer to view the lakes, and the extenſive proſpect from the top of Skiddaw-hill.

The next morning being cloudy, I was prevented of a ſight of Skiddaw-hill, the greater part of it being covered with clouds: It is ſaid to be the higheſt mountain in the iſland;

its

its perpendicular height above the furface of the lake is 2560 feet.

About three miles from Kefwick, a fine fertile vale prefents itfelf to the view; and the landfcape is greatly improved by the advantageous fituation of the beholder; the road along which he is then travelling being cut out of the fide of a high, barren, mountain. The vale, which is level, and between three and four miles round, is on the right-hand fide of the way, and is bounded by high mountains, and Derwent and Baffenthwaite Lake. Skiddaw is one of thefe, and is now juft on your right hand; and behind it a part of Derwent Lake may be feen. The boundary mountain on the farther fide of the vale, is not, I was told, near fo high

high as Skiddaw; but that right opposite to Skiddaw, is nearly of the same height with it; and behind this opposite mountain a part of Bassenthwaite Lake is to be seen. This distribution is remarkably uniform and immense.

"T' engage the Thought, and please the ravish'd Eye."

And while variety, uniformity, and immensity employ the sight, pleasure and a reverend horror at once possess the mind.

Cockermouth stands somewhat low. The houses are chiefly white, being rough-cast, that is, dashed with lime and small stones; and are covered with slate. It is a pretty neat town, and has a market on Mondays.

Mondays. A confiderable trade is carried on here with Ireland: Butter and hides are two principal articles imported—and perhaps a bottle of French brandy may fometimes find its way over.

I am, dear Sir,

Yours, &c.

# WHITEHAVEN.

SIR,

AT three o'clock in the afternoon I attained Whitehaven. This place has, at first sight, a very singular appearance; though you are long in expectation of it before you do see it. It stands low, between two promontories; and, at the first view, which is not above a hundred yards distant from the skirts of the town, you are presented with nothing but the blue slate coverings of of the houfes, and fmoke.—Juft as you begin to defcend the brow of the hill, ftand two fmall conical fpires, encompaffed by a wall, clofe to the road, on the right hand: They are almoft clofe together, and are of the fame height, each of about forty-five feet, and on either Apex is a neat gilt vane. They are called the Tobacco-pipes,—are hollow, and are for the purpofe of burning the damaged tobacco in.

In Whitehaven are three churches, or rather chapels of eafe, the mother church being that at St. Bees. The old church, as it is ufually called, is dedicated to St. John, the other two to the Trinity and St. James. In the old church is an organ, which ftands at the eaft-end, over the altar-table;

table; and against the wall, above the table, and below the organ, is a piece of painting, reprefenting our Saviour eating the laſt ſupper with his Apoſtles. Our Saviour is in an attitude as if juſt riſing off his ſeat, and reaching out a piece of bread to one of his difciples, uttering thefe words, as expreffed by the motto, *" This do in Remembrance of me."*— St. James's church is the moſt modern, and is very beautiful.

The town is very regularly built, and, as I mentioned to you before, lies low, between two ridges of mountains, which ſtretch into the ſea, and theſe ridges include the haven. The ſtreets are in general broad and ſtraight, and moſtly interſect each other at right angles. The market-

## KILKENNY. 29

market-place is pretty large. The chief market-day is Thursday. Beef and mutton were selling at threepence and threepence-halfpenny a pound;—Fowls, in general, cheap;—Herrings, six and seven a penny, and, I was told, they were sometimes ten or twelve a penny. Potatoes were at twopence-halfpenny a stone, Butter, sevenpence and eightpence a pound, of sixteen ounces: Fruit and Nuts were in great plenty; Apples at sixpence a hoop, or quarter of the old peck, that is at the rate of eightpence a Winchester peck;—Nuts were at about the same price.

There are many coal-pits near the town, and a great number of ships are constantly employed in carrying the coals to different ports in Ireland. The

The harbour is well secured, and much improved by five piers or ramparts, which project into the sea. Some of these piers are, from morning till night, crouded with coal-carts; the two furthest are generally lined with loaded ships.

When any person dies here, it is customary for the common bellman to patrol the streets, with the following invitatory cry;—"*All friends and neighbours are desired to attend the corps of —— of ——street, to —— church this evening: The corps will be taken out at —— o'clock.*" During my stay, which was about nine days, many children died of the small-pox: I once saw five corps together in the old church. Inoculation was formerly much practised in this quarter,

till

till a few years ago, when three or four dying in that fatal diforder, after they had been inoculated, it was entirely laid afide; and the people now choofe to fubmit to Providence rather than the operation.—One day I attended the corps of a very worthy gentleman to the old church, who died of a more extraordinary, and perhaps not lefs fatal, difeafe than the fmall-pox. He had been brought up to the fea, and had conftantly adhered to his vocation, till about fix months before his death, when a relation leaving him an eftate of upwards of an hundred pounds a-year, he threw off his healthful employment, and commenced a gentleman. Though it did not appear that he had, in the leaft, applied himfelf to the deftructive and fafhionable appendages

dages of that calling; nor at all given himself to luxury, or any way devoted to pleasure, according to the frequent acceptation of that word, but only to ease, and ease proved mortal. He was much lamented.

---

I have now given you all that I noticed on this side the Irish sea, and, perhaps, more than is worthy your notice: but I could not well restrain my pen from relating all that I had thought either worth my while to remark on paper, or treasure up in my mind for your entertainment.

I am, Sir,

Yours, &c.

**LETTER**

## LETTER III.

*From WHITEHAVEN, to SKERRIES in IRELAND.*

SIR,

ON Saturday the 12th of October, in the morning, the wind became favourable, and we set sail, in company with twenty or twenty-one others, twelve of which, including ourselves, were bound to Dublin. The sea was very calm, and the gale very moderate. About three o'clock in the afternoon the wind changed, and became contrary, and continued so till about five the next morning. At sun-rising I came upon deck to look about me, and a delightful look it was; particularly as the land we were then close in with, I supposed to be Ireland, not knowing that the wind had changed;—but, sad illusive sight!—for the land, on inquiry, proved to be the Isle of Man.——We came close up to Ramsey. The people seemed to have just risen, and to be making on their fires, by the great quantity of smoke that issued from the chimneys.——In the afternoon we passed by Douglas, the chief port in the island. On the east-side of it is a large tract of seemingly good land, neatly laid out, and apparently well fenced. I could discern many new inclosures all along the coast. The interior part is very

mountainous

mountainous and irregular, and the higher lands appear to be quite barren.

On Sunday night the wind blew strong and contrary, but on Monday morning it became more calm, though still continued unkind.—— We were tugged about in this little space, between the Isle of Man and Ireland, till Wednesday the 16th in the afternoon, when, the wind blowing afresh the Captain thought it best to run into a harbour in Ireland called Skerries, which is about five leagues to the North of Dublin harbour. From Sunday till this time, I had been almost wholly confined to my cabin, there amusing myself as well as I could, or as circumstances would permit. One agreeable comfort however often attended me, and that was a melodious fellow paſſenger, who ſeemed, by his cheerfulneſs, to have nothing to dread from the elements. Whether the ſea was rough or ſmooth,—the wind Eaſt or Weſt— he was ſtill in tune—his bellows blew always the ſame. This good company was more than a mere put-off, I aſſure you—it really was entertaining to me to hear the man bellowing, as it were, at the clamorous ocean. His ſongs I ſeldom knew, nor, indeed, could I always diſtinctly hear his tune, though he evidently endeavoured, as far as he was able, to keep up a counter-plea with the noiſome waves.—In ſhort—He was every way adapted to my wiſhes, and particularly to my preſent ſituation; and if I found any inconveniency in his company, I am certain it originated

nated within my own breaſt:—Perhaps I might unawares covet his difpoſition, but that was wrong in me, and no fault in my companion. He was a man for either land or water,—he was any man's man,—he was a man for the world.

Sir,

Yours, &c.

## LETTER IV.

*SKERRIES, in IRELAND.*

SIR,

AFTER we came to anchor in the harbour of Skerries my floating prison abated its giddy motion,—all was steady and quiet,—and we seemed as if sincerely at peace with the rugged waves. In this agreeable situation, I ventured to peep out, and crawl upon deck once more.—I was charmed with the verdant prospect:—Had I had nothing but the appearance of terrestrial objects to estimate the season by, I should have

have dated my memoranda that day, April the twenty-fifth.—It was beautiful even to a dizzy head. The view was extenſive, both up into the country, and on both ſides of the bay, and included two gentlemen's houſes, which, being white, made ſome addition to the landſcape.

After I had done gazing at the country, I found other objects to amuſe me, which before I had overlooked: Theſe were the fiſhing-wherries (ſo they call them) plying about in almoſt all directions, and taking up their lines. I counted twenty-eight in motion, beſides thoſe lying in the harbour, cloſe by a pier that projected from the end of the town. They appeared juſt like ſo many Swallows ſkimming over a pond,

pond, and preying upon the flies. The bay abounds with fish.

All this time I stood—I felt an emotion within me, expressing a desire for something—or to be somewhere,—but I could not be diverted from my entertainments—I could not allow myself time to consider what it was I would be at. However, when the ecstacy was about over, and I was turning to my cabin-stairs—I sighed at the thought—That I should be again committed to a merciless element, which I looked upon as a professed enemy, ever gaping to devour me,—and which, from the treatment I had already met with, I could not persuade myself at all to rely on.—I cast about again,—and, at last, I plainly wished to be on on shore. The Captain, who, I dare say, had long before read my desire very plainly in my countenance, was very civil, and said he would go with me. I accepted his kind offer, and we set sail, in a four-oar boat, for the town of Skerries.—I have often heard it said of a person, when in difficulties, or under some oppression, figuratively termed a frying-pan, in endeavouring to extricate himself, often falls into greater troubles, or as the figure expresses it,—leaps into the fire;—this was exactly my case: For in the way we got entangled among the fishing-lines, which drew the Wherries about us on all sides, and so exasperated the churlish fellows, that I would not have insured our cargo for less than ninety-nine per Cent.—In this excursion (I forgot

got to tell you before) I was attended by my former jovial companion;—he, happy man! bore all with his usual equanimity of disposition,—not the least appearance of dread was to be seen about him;—happy man, indeed!—Who would not have coveted his disposition? We arrived at last safe along the side of the pier, where a number of men were gathered together, chiefly, I suppose, to look about them, to see what passed, and how trade went on. They seemed to be mostly of the amphibious kind,—and, upon my word, some of them were brawny fellows. They all advanced towards us as we stepped out of the boat. We inquired of them for the best Inn in the town,—but, instead of giving any answer, they in turn asked of us an account

of

of our voyage;—we entreated them to attend to our inquiry,—telling them, that I wanted to be at a houſe where I might be accommodated with good lodgings, and a horſe in the morning to Dublin.—At laſt one of them bawled out—" I have a horſe."—I went up to him, and aſked him ſome queſtions about his horſe,—but, after a few frivolous interrogations, he very heartily told me—he would not let me have his horſe, becauſe he did not know me. This made me recollect perfectly where I was,—and I could not forbear laughing:—Paddy grinn'd—and I made off. By this time the Captain, at a little diſtance from me, had found one more kindly diſpoſed than many of the reſt, and who could talk plainer Engliſh than any

I had

I had conversed with;—he came up, and, in an honest rustic tone, said he would go with me to an house where I might have any thing I wanted. This was good hearing.— We followed him. The first house he stopt at had but a very poor appearance;—however we got into it. The inside afforded an old and a young woman,—both were very civil. We got some ale---they had nothing better;---it was one-penny a pint, which is the common price all over Ireland: It is seldom strong, yet has, in general, an agreeable taste. The old woman was sitting by a few embers in the hearth, darning her stockings; the young lady kept moving about the house, and was no mean sight---only her head was rather too high for her roof.---

We

We set out in pursuit of something better. Our leader conducted us to another house——worse and worse ——this would never do. We proceeded, and came to a third. The Captain advised me to heave out anchor;—I did—I made it do—though it was no hotel, I assure you. The first thing I met with was the top of the door-frame,—it made much too free with my forehead.——The mistress, however, was a good decent-looking woman.

I settled my account with the Captain, and, in a few minutes, he, with the passenger and men, returned to the ship.—I got shaven, and a clean shirt on, and I was as happy as a king.

I was now left alone with my landlady, and two barefoot children her offspring. Her husband and two servant-girls, she said, were at the farm taking up potatoes, and a servant-boy was threshing in the barn behind the house. She very kindly informed me, that she sold Rum, Brandy, Gin, and Whiskey. I desired her to bring me a *pot* of her Whiskey:———she looked—and muttered—and stammered---I perceived she did not understand me;———at length, by halfing, and quartering, we demonstrated, that my *pot* was equal to her *noggin*. I got a noggin of *plain* Whiskey;———but she said ---Gentlemen always drank *currant* Whiskey.———This is a spirituous liquor made from malt: The plain sort tastes somewhat like Gin, especially

cially that which is made in those parts where Juniper-berries are to be had. The Currant-whiskey is made by infusing Currants in the plain Whiskey.——Her prices were about the same, as I afterwards found, with those in Dublin.

In the evening our landlord appeared, with a cargo of Potatoes---- a good looking man indeed he was, and talked good English. He certainly had been a gentleman's servant,---he had travelled.

Much company came in,——but they did not in the least disturb me. The kitchen (if you please) was set about with a double row of forms, and on these the guests sat. I was fixed on a solid log of wood, in the nook

nook, by (or rather in) the range—for it was fair weather. Our fire confisted mostly of wood, with a little coal. A crane was fixed to a piece of wood in the chimney above, and turned on the hearth-stone below, and supplied the place of a range-crook. The mistress bid one of the servants get straw, and begin to prepare supper. The girl obeyed, and soon had the house half filled with straw. She then filled a large iron pot with potatoes, and hanging it on the crane, turned the crane and pot about into the corner or nook opposite to that wherein I was sitting.——— She piled up the straw, and drew it near the pot, and seating herself upon it, pulled out a little at a time from under her, and supplied a blaze upon the pot, till the potatoes were enough,

enough, which was, I obferved, juft when the ftraw was all confumed.——Supper was turned out into a large tub, and they fettled themfelves orderly about it, in the middle of the floor.

A little after fupper, the gentry on the forms began to be merry. Every one fang a fong—fome two——but not one word could I underftand——nor was I much delighted with their mufic:——I know not whether the ingenious northern Tourift would have been delighted with fuch melody.

In the midft of this jollity I recollected I had not provided a horfe for my intended journey in the morning to Dublin. I fent for a perfon who had

had horses. He came,—but not a syllable of his answers did I understand. He had lately come out of the North of Ireland, where the lower class of people know very little of the English language.——This scene gave those about us great pleasure,——they laughed with much glee at our perpetual interrogations, and the uselessness of our tongues.—— The landlord came to us, and was kind enough to mediate as interpreter. We soon agreed on a price;—— but, on his hearing me name Kilkenny, he enquired whether I was going there,——on being answered yes,——the bargain was void:—— No such thing as he would lend his horse to one that was going beyond Dublin.——This usage, you may be sure, nettled me not a little—I could have

have fwore at the old fellow.———I applied to another, of more faith than the former, and was fortunate enough to fucceed. Now, per agreement, my nag was to be equipt with a leather faddle, a bridle of the fame, and fuitable girths. You will here fay—" What others couldft thou have had?" I will tell you,——a faddle, bridle, Stirrups, crupper, all of ftraw, might have been my portion,—though indeed, for a pot extraordinary, I might perhaps have procured a cord-bridle, and cord ftirrups: and the very next day convinced me, that, with thefe accoutrements, I fhould not have been of the leaft magnitude among my brethren, however fingular I might appear in my own eyes; for the greater number of perfons I met travelling on horfeback, before I came

into

into the poſt-road, had either no better, or none at all.

I prepared for bed.——After I had got into my room, and had ſhut the door, I found it rather airy, and taking the candle in my hand, took a ſurvey of my apartment. There were two openings, which, ſome time or other, had been windows; for the one had two panes of glaſs in it,— the other one,—the ſpaces being ſtopt up with pieces of board, clouts, &c. —This was frightful indeed—I could not refrain from pitying myſelf,— but all was in vain—it was my deſtined habitation.——I laid me down in peace, in hope to find ſome reſt, —but that was far from me.——The bed was too quick—I ſcratch'd—I turn'd—and turn'd and ſcratch'd again

gain—and wished for morning a hundred times before it came.——At length bright Sol appeared through the chinks of the windows.—I got up—ordered my breakfast and horse, and then took a walk out into the town. It was a charming fine morning to be the seventeenth of October.

Sir,

Yours, &c.

LETTER

# LETTER V.

*SKERRIES,————continued.*

SIR,

THERE are many small Islands in and near the Bay: I could see four from the town. On one, which is that nearest the town, are the remains of a church, dedicated to their Patron, St. Patrick. This Island is said to be the first place on which the saint landed on his arrival in Ireland, which was near the end of the fourth century. The Church is also said to have been built under his

his own immediate infpection, at which time the ifland was parted from the main land by only a fmall ftream of water at fpring tides, and then paffable on foot. But the faint had not divined well, for now it is impaffable at the loweft ebb of the tide, and, on that account, the facred pile was long ago neceffarily abandoned, and little more of it at prefent remains than the bare name.— There is now a church in the town called St. Patrick's new church.

This place fupplies the country, for more than twenty miles round, with fifh, which is caught in great abundance. Dublin is about twenty miles hence, and is fupplied chiefly with that article from this place, which is conveyed in *cars*.

The

The houses are low, some of them are extremely low, which latter, in Ireland, are denominated *cabins*. They are situated, with respect to each other, very irregularly: For it can hardly be said that there is a single street in the whole town, though it consists of upwards of a hundred houses.

These *cars*, just mentioned, are small carriages, having two low wheels of about twenty-two inches diameter; they are drawn by a single horse. The wheels are thin round blocks of wood, sometimes tired with iron, and are fixed fast to the axle-tree. In Dublin the wheels turn with an iron axle-tree, which being continued out on the outsides of the wheels, the car rests on those

continued

continued parts. But in the country the wheels are moſtly fixed at the extremities of a wooden axle-tree, and the body of the car lies upon it on two places between the wheels.--- It is to be hoped that the country-people, for the ſake of both themſelves and their horſes, will, in time, come into the Dublin method of conſtructing their cars, and that, perhaps, may be improved.

It is very common for the lower ſort of people to join and hire a car when going a journey, or taking a jaunt of pleaſure, laying ſtraw, a mat, or ſometimes a bed on the bottom of it, to make their ſeats more comfortable and eaſy. I have numbered ſix women on a car, with their legs hanging down within a few inches

inches of the ground, and moving no faster than a person on foot. I have seen a grocer's wife mounted on one of those humble vehicles,—and a beautiful woman she was,—I never saw such condescension in England.—The inhabitants of Yarmouth indeed have carriages much resembling the Irish cars, which they generally dignify by the name of coaches. There are numbers of them employed in carrying goods about the town, in the same manner as the cars are used in Dublin. In Summer, particularly during the bathing season, these *coaches* are let out to company who visit the town, and choose an excursion, in parties, to the fort upon the Deanes, or into the country; but then the carriages for these purposes are mostly painted,

some

some red, some green, some blue, which renders them much superior, in point of grandeur, to the humble Irish car.

I shall just give you a description of an Irish *cabin*, and a few other particulars, and then proceed on my way to Dublin.

The Irish cabins are built of earth, or muddy clay, wrought into the consistence of mortar, and are always well thatched. Sometimes stakes are fixed into the ground, to support the walls, and as a firm foundation to the building. Round the stakes the architect sheds alternate Strata of mortar and sods, till he attains the height of five or six feet above the floor or first story,—then timbers,—

covers in, and the fabric is completed. Few of them have either window or chimney, or any other aperture but that which serves the purpose of a common entrance—people, poultry, and pigs, often lodge and feed together under one of these roofs.

I am, dear Sir,

Yours, &c.

LETTER

# LETTER VI.

*A general account of IRELAND;—its divisions, subdivisions, or counties, parishes, measures, coins, &c.*

---

SIR,

BEFORE I advance further in my journey, I will lay before you the following tables, which I have extracted from a larger one in Doctor Trusler's Chronology.

Ireland is divided into four large Provinces, *Ulster, Leinster, Mun-*

*ster*, and *Connaught*. Ulster comprehends nine counties, Leinster twelve, Munster six, and Connaught five. The number of acres, houses, (as they were numbered in 1766) and Parishes, in each province and county is as follows.

| Counties in Ulster. | Irish Plantation Acres. | Houses. | Parishes. |
|---|---|---|---|
| ULSTER. | 2836837 | 128983 | 365 |
| 1 Antrim | 383020 | 20738 | 56 |
| 2 Armagh | 170620 | 13125 | 49 |
| 3 Cavan | 274800 | 9268 | 37 |
| 4 Down | 344658 | 26090 | 72 |
| 5 Donegal | 630157 | 12357 | 40 |
| 6 Fermanagh | 224807 | 5674 | 19 |
| 7 Londonderry | 251510 | 14528 | 38 |
| 8 Monaghan | 170090 | 10658 | 24 |
| 9 Tyrone | 387175 | 16545 | 30 |

| Counties in Leinster. | Irish Plantation Acres. | Houses. | Parishes |
|---|---|---|---|
| LEINSTER. | 2642958 | 127901 | 858 |
| 1 Catherlough | 116900 | 5444 | 42 |
| 2 Dublin | 123784 | 23103 | 87 |
| 3 Kildare | 228590 | 8555 | 100 |
| 4 Kilkenny | 287650 | 13231 | 96 |
| 5 King's County | 257510 | 9294 | 56 |
| 6 Longford | 134700 | 6057 | 24 |
| 7 Louth | 111180 | 8151 | 50 |
| 8 Meath | 326480 | 14000 | 139 |
| 9 Queen'a County | 238415 | 11226 | 30 |
| 10 Westmeath | 249943 | 9621 | 62 |
| 11 Wexford | 315936 | 11438 | 109 |
| 12 Wicklow | 252410 | 7781 | 54 |

| Counties in Munster. | Irish Plantation Acres. | Houses. | Parishes. |
|---|---|---|---|
| MUNSTER. | 3289932 | 117197 | 740 |
| 1 Clare | 428187 | 11381 | 76 |
| 2 Cork | 991010 | 47.334 | 232 |
| 3 Kerry | 636905 | 12112 | 84 |
| 4 Limerick | 375320 | 19380 | 130 |
| 5 Tipperary | 599500 | 18057 | 147 |
| 6 Waterford | 259010 | 8933 | 71 |

| Counties in Connaught. | Irish Plantation Acres. | Houses. | Parishes. |
|---|---|---|---|
| CONNAUGHT. | 2272915 | 49966 | 330 |
| 1 Galway | 775525 | 15576 | 136 |
| 2 Leitrim | 206830 | 5156 | 21 |
| 3 Mayo | 724640 | 15089 | 73 |
| 4 Roscommon | 324370 | 8216 | 59 |
| 5 Sligo | 241550 | 5292 | 41 |
| Total of Counties in Ireland. | Total of Acres in Ireland. | Total of Houses. | Total of Parishes. |
| 32 | 11042642 | 424047 | 2293 |

Five

Five acres Irish are equal to eight acres fifteen perches and one hundred and five parts English. The Irish measure with *seven*, the English with *five and a half* yards to the pole.

In Ireland two shillings is paid yearly for every hearth or fire-place; but they pay no land-tax yet.

An Irish mile is six thousand seven hundred and twenty feet, or ten furlongs and one hundred and twenty feet; whence eleven Irish miles are exactly equal to fourteen English miles.

An English shilling is thirteen Irish pence; therefore a guinea is one pound two shillings and nine-
pence

pence Irish, at Par. And this leads me to observe to you the great scarcity of copper coin in Ireland, which is entirely owing to the vast quantity of that species exported thence to England, where it is well known to be a load, at least, if not a nuisance to the public. Every sailor, before he leaves Ireland, gleans up all the halfpence he possibly can, for the sake of the penny in thirteen profit. And thus the public of two nations are injured by the emolument of a few individuals.

The want of small currency, which is particularly felt on the East coast, and other places frequented by English ships, has induced many tradesmen in these parts to strike copper coins, which pass very currently in their

their own neighbourhood. On the one fide, "*I promife to pay the bearer* (one, two, three, or four) *pence on demand.* P——— O——— 1771, and, on the reverfe, is the Coiner's fign, and the value, as 1 P. 2 P. or 3 P. &c.

"The want of fmall change (in 1727) was fo great that feveral perfons were obliged to make copper and filver tokens called *Traders*, which they paffed as promiffory notes among their workmen, cuftomers and neighbours, and each has the name of the perfon who iffued them, with the place of his abode. Some of thefe were ftruck at Armagh, Belfaft, Dromore, Lurgan, Portadown and Dublin."—See the *Account of Irifh coins*, page 61.

This popular grievance might easily be redressed, and it is much to be wished that it were.

Sir,

Yours, &c.

## LETTER VII.

*From SKERRIES to DUBLIN.*

SIR,

I WILL now proceed on my journey.—Having got a pretty comfortable breakfast, and part of a noggin of Whiskey, I mounted my steed, and set out for Dublin. The distance is seventeen (Irish) miles, nearly. I had about four miles to ride before I came into the North post-road. I had never travelled upon a finer road in England than even the former four miles were; and the post-road was much broader,

'and,

and, in general, better. Indeed all the roads I came in, or interfected, were very good, and remarkaby ftraight; but this North-road is allowed, at prefent, to be the beft in Ireland.—In travelling in one direction, you meet with only one tollgate in the fame county, and that feldom demands more of you than one-penny a horfe; except indeed in what is called the Circular-road about Dublin; of which I fhall give you a fhort account when I come to that city.

In the firft four miles the inclofures are moftly fmall, few exceed three acres, and are feparated by mounds of earth only; though fometimes, they are ftuck, in a flight manner, with Gorfe, Willows, &c.
Great

Great quantities of fine potatoes, and some wheat and barley, are produced in this quarter. The corn and hay harvests, I observed, were about at the same time. Many fields of both were then standing out. The corn they pile up in a conical form, in the manner of the English stacks; a day or two before it is led, they spread it out, then bind it up fast in sheaves, and lead it together, and put it into stack.— I conclude, from this observation, That the harvest is much later in these parts than it is in most counties of England; and, from what intelligence I could collect, they reap as early in the county of Dublin as in any other in the whole Island. This must render their harvest precarious, and the grain often not very wholesome.—As I advanced towards Dublin, agriculture began to have a better aspect, industry began to shew better handy-work, and improvements in general seemed to be better known and more practised. Some quickset-hedges were now to be met with; tho' indolence here and there marred the prospect with fences of earth, and others of stones piled up without any mortar, like those in Westmoreland, Cumberland, &c. Many of the quicksets I observed to be in a very thriving state, such as were not so had been neglected. The Hawthorn I know will not endure the salt-water spray, but it may be reared in most soils remote from the sea. And I well remember I did not discover one single acre of barren land in all the way.

The

The sides of the road are well planted with houses, many of which are cabins:—What is saved in tolls may be readily disposed of in charity, if the traveller has got a single spark of humanity in his breast. The objects that came crawling to me from the cabins would have softened the most stony heart. I must own at least, I could not withstand their attacks,—every feature plainly shewed poverty, and humbly asked my charity:—I gave them—and that relieved both them and me.

Sir,

Yours affectionately,

**LETTER**

# LETTER VIII.

*DUBLIN, the Capital of Ireland.*

SIR,

About two o'clock in the afternoon I arrived at Dublin. Being, from my circumstances, obliged to make some stay here, I had an opportunity of seeing most parts of the city; and such particulars and occurrences as I judge sufficient to amuse you in a leisure hour, I will inform you of. And, if at any time I chance to run into Mr. Twiss's track, which I believe I cannot possibly avoid, I hope you will forgive me, me, as you may be affured I will cautioufly fhun *that*, as well as every other beaten path which I know of, or which I can by any means clearly difcern. But this I beg you will remember, that to write nothing but what is new, efpecially in giving the geographical defcription of this capital, fituated but a few ftrides from us, cannot be done,—I dare fay you will not expect; yet novelty, or new defcriptions, or new objects, ought to be our chief aim, I acknowledge, and then the better we fucceed in fuch defiderata, the more will our labours be regarded and read, and their merit will be meafured by the fcale of general importance, or by the line of public entertainment. But to leave this digreffion;——Dublin ftands on a pretty extenfive plain. The laft eight

eight miles I had travelled were nearly on a level with the city; and the country, for fix or feven miles to the fouth, is exceedingly even, at which diftance are a ridge of mountains extending about twelve miles, from the mouth of the bay into the country. The whole of this plain is very fertile, and the fituation of the city is generally efteemed falubrious.

The city is divided into two almoft equal parts by the river Liffey, which forms itfelf into a bay about a mile below the town. A few fine clofes have been lately acquired from the fouth-fide of the bay, clofe by Irifh-Town; and it was then in agitation to proceed in like manner further down the bay, on the fame fide, to dyke off a much larger tract.

A

A little below Irish-Town, and nearly two miles from the city, in the bay, stands the Light-house or Pigeon-house, as it is commonly called. The entrance into this harbour is extremely beautiful, and is said to be exceeded in grandeur by the harbour of Naples only. But the bar, which is near the Pigeon-house, renders the passage very incommodious, so that ships of any burthen dare not venture in.

The city is nearly circular, and is about eight miles in circumference. Each part, on either side of the river, is encompassed by a broad walk, named the Circular-road. This road is much frequented by the better sort of people, on foot, on horseback, and in carriages. It was made for the purpose

purpose of furnishing a convenient airing. The money that is collected at the several toll-gates on the road is applied totally to keeping it in repair.——It undoubtedly affords an agreeable jaunt, but the account of so many robberies committed on it, rather allays the pleasure which it would otherwise give.—The north and south parts of the town are connected by five bridges. Essex-bridge is the principal; it is situated to the east of the others, or is next towards the bay.—An application was lately made to parliament for leave to build another, to the east of Essex-bridge; where it is thought by many another is much wanted; but the bill was thrown out, on the supposition that it would be more an obstacle to trade than a convenience to the public:

# KILKENNY. 81

public.—There are two or three ferry-boats constantly passing below Essex-bridge.

There are two cathedrals, and eighteen parish-churches, besides several chapels, and meeting-houses, for the Dutch protestants, presbyterians, quakers, and methodists, in this city; there are also sixteen Roman-catholic chapels. The cathedrals are St. Patrick's church, and Christ's church. Both resemble the cathedrals in England, but neither are near so beautiful nor so large as those of York or Durham. Swift was Dean of St. Patrick's, and was buried in it. I was but once in it, and that was at the time of divine service. The very first moment I entered the choir, I fixed my eye on

the

the prieſt—" Dearly beloved Roger" leaped inſtantly into my head.——— Poor Swift! thought I, that was once thy place;——I caſt ſteadily about for Roger,——but, in a little time, I recollected my miſtake——— the beloved Roger did not belong here.

The firſt Sunday after my arrival, I attended divine ſervice, in the evening, at Chriſt's church; it was performed in candle-light. This cathedral is more beautiful than St. Patrick's. The choir is narrow;— there are three row⬛⬛s on each ſide, and the diſta⬛⬛⬛e, between them is not mo⬛⬛ feet. It has galleries on both ſide⬛ The organ is placed in a gall⬛⬛ on the one ſide of the choir near the altar-table.

## KILKENNY. 83

table. The principal fingers go up into this gallery when the anthem is given out;—this was much the beſt chorus I heard in Ireland.

Both theſe cathedrals are on the South-ſide of the river. The Round-church (one ſo called) is on the ſame ſide. It is, as the name expreſſes it, really round, and is very convenient for performing their oratorios in.

The modern built churches have neither ſpires nor ſteeples, and ſome of the o̴̴̴̴̴ have had their ſpires pulled ̴̴̴̴̴ The Iriſh ſeem to be terri̴̴̴ of thunder.

The palace of St. Sepulchre, the univerſity, and the parliament-houſe, are in the South part of the town.

The university confists of a single college, dedicated to the Trinity. The front has a grand appearance. Indeed its fituation adds much to its grandeur. The ftreet leading to its front is named College-green. This ftreet regularly widens as you approach the college, and, at laft, terminates in a triangular opening; the college, which is now right facing you, being one of the three fides, a row of very genteel houfes forms the fide on the right hand, and the parliament-houfe takes up the greater part of the fide on t̄̄̄̄ and an equeftrian ftatue of William III. is placed nearly i̅̅̅̅le of the fpace.

The parliament-houfe is very beautiful, and is looked upon as one of the

the chiefeſt ornaments of the city. Its front is of the Ionic Order, and, in general, is well executed. Its portico is of a ſingular conſtruction, and is affirmed to be the moſt elegant in Europe.

But the fineſt and moſt elegant piece of architecture in Dublin, is the Lying-in-hoſpital. Strangers are uſually led here to view the city from the towers, which appears indeed very beautiful; but the proſpect takes in the bay, and a great part of the adjacent country, along with the city, which together form a very fine landſcape.

The ſquare called St. Stephen's-green, is ſituated a little to the ſouth of the college. It is the largeſt ſquare in Europe,—the four sides together make nearly a mile. The interior part is surrounded by a low wall, between which and the houses, about thirty feet are left for a coach-road. On the inside of the wall is a broad gravel-walk, planted on either side with trees, called *beau*'s-*walk*;—the name is exceedingly pertinent and expressive. Beaux and belles, and their peculiar stratagems, are here frequently displayed. I have seen the walk so thick with these toys frisking about, that a *man* could hardly pass along for them.—You'll say—A *man* has no business on their premisses,—True,—but there can be little harm in his taking a look at things professedly designed for show,—and, generally speaking, there cannot be any great crime in his peeping into

into any other species of folly, provided he is secured from dipping into it. The wisest, and perhaps the best, of men, are at certain times agreeably relaxed and entertained with mere trifles,—with a harlequin—with a merry-Andrew——with punch and his wife—and why not with a beau and a belle?

There are two theatres-royal, and many hospitals, besides that already mentioned, as St. Patrick's hospital, for lunatics and ideots, the Old-man's hospital, and some others. St. Patrick's was founded by the celebrated Dean Swift.—There is also a new exchange building, which, from the plan, the superb manner of execution, and the pleasant situation, promises fair to become, in a little time,

the

the finest building, and the chief embellishment in the city of Dublin.

The barracks are in the North part of the city, and at the Western extremity, near to the side of the river. They consist of three squares, or rather imperfect squares, each wanting its South side. They are capable of containing six Thousand men.

To the West of the barracks is Phœnix park,—a place of great resort in fine weather.—In this park is a fort.

Sir,

Yours, &c.

## LETTER IX.

*DUBLIN,--------continued.*

SIR,

THE out-skirts of Dublin consist mostly of cabins. Each cabin has generally a small piece of ground belonging to it, which produces a few potatoes, cabbages, and onions, the constant food of the Irish poor all the year round. Flesh seldom enters their miserable dwellings,—and bread not often. But whiskey they will have—they think it almost impossible to subsist without it:——It is their darling, and their

their ruin,—it contributes much to their prefent deplorable ftate of ftupidity and poverty. Their faculties are benumbed by the extravagant ufe of it, and their families are thereby plunged to the very bottom of diftrefs. It is the parent of that favage, brutal temper, fo confpicious in the common Irifh, and is certainly the foundation of all their peculiar calamities and misfortunes. In fhort —It renders their minds unapt for ferious thinking, and their bodies inactive in ufeful labour;——reduces them far below the dignity of their nature,—and, but too often, urges to fuch offences as juftly open the folding arms of the avenging laws to hug them into endlefs eternity.

In the year 1749 it was computed, that

that in the city and liberties of Dublin there were two thoufand alehoufes, three hundred taverns, and twelve hundred brandy-fhops. In 1776 the number of houfes in Dublin was thirteen thoufand one hundred and ninety-four.

I was informed, that, in Ulfter, and fome parts of Connaught, where whifkey is remarkably cheap, it was very common for the people to fup whifkey to their potatoes, in the manner the Englifh eat bread and milk; but that the children, while young, had water in it, and, as they grew up, the water was gradually leffened, and, at laft, wholly left off. ——This, if it be true, is a practice greatly to be lamented; and, confidering it as a cuftom, the people themfelves themselves are much to be pitied.

The better sort of people in Dublin have much civility in them, which they bestow very lavishly on Englishmen, I experienced their kindness, and, with much gratitude, now recall it to my mind. They are generally free, or rather forward, in their talking, and are utter strangers to those hesitations and apologies which are obtruded so often upon us in companies in England. Reserve they seem not to have any idea of;—nor does the Irishman suffer much by opening the window of his breast. He is generally acute in argument and common conversation.———A *Bull* to be sure, is a large animal,——— apt to produce a bellow,———easily, and often too critically, observed;

and

and always largely applied.——
But there is a kind of readiness in
his conception, and an easy vivacity in his turn, which elevate him
far above a sulky mastiff, or a busy
cur.——

The trading part of the people
seem to pique themselves much upon
the fairness of their dealing. I alwas observed them offended when
I bid them less than they had set
upon any goods,——the least hint
of over-charging will cloud their eyes.
——I went into a shop in Leighlinbridge, and desired to look at some
pocket handkerchiefs the mistress
of the shop did not talk over plain
English, nor did she understand every
word I said:——She perceived I was
a foreigner, and, very familiarly, inquired

quired my country;—I told her. She pointed to another sort, which she said would suit me better,——the price of these was so much— I bid her something less for four or five.——This puckered her brow a little;—she would not take any less if I took ever so many,——did I think she meant to cheat me?—She would assure me she practised no such mean methods!——and thus she went on for some time,——not a word could I get in with her,—at last however I drew up an excuse—squeezing in all the reason I could muster—(which then, by the by, was not over savoury;) It had a good effect—it produced a calm. She then very cooly informed me —That if it had been that woman, —nodding to one going out of the shop

shop-door,—she would have asked more by so much;——that she believed the English to be generally sincere and upright, and so concluded that they would be greatly displeased, and not less surprized at being imposed upon by so near a neighbour.——I here leave the inference to your own judgment, you will easily determine the bounds of this partial uprightness,—though I am persuaded a small allowance was due to a soothing politeness, which they have borrowed from another neighbouring nation.

The Irish seem to be very attentive to the education of their females. In the mercantile class, we frequently find the women keeping the books, while the men are employed

ployed in the other ordinary bufinefs of the fhop. This is alfo
common in France, and probably
the Irifh have had the cuftom
thence.

Being three or four times in a
printer's office, I found him one
day at work printing Eliza's Letters
to Yorick, for many of the boofellers
in Dublin, on a tolerable good paper,
and with a pretty neat type.—A cor-
rector attended the prefs.

On inquiry, I found Triftram-
Shandy met with great fale in Ireland; but Yorick's Sermons were
not near fo well known,—nor was
the Sentimental Journey in great
eftimation among them.—Thus we
find the moft valuable productions
do

" plebeian females." This she contended, was aimed obliquely at the ladies, or at least they were included, (—I believe they might—) but she could not support her opinion with any tolerable arguments, so it dropt. —It is more than probable, that the lady, though very sensible, was resolved to take part with her own dear country, and so had laid hold of those few innocent lines whereby to defend her cause.

I am, dear Sir,

Yours, &c.

LETTER

## LETTER X.

*DUBLIN,——continued.*

SIR,

THE lower sort of people in the outer streets of Dublin, are seldom loaded with shoes and stockings, especially the females and Children. I have noticed more than one young woman, with a head-dress imitative of the ton——four or five rings on one hand——and not in the meanest gown——with one hand behind tucking up her petticoat——without either stocking or shoe. I have also often noticed boys in ruffled shirts,

shirts, and otherwise neatly clad, going barefoot.

There are many goats kept in Dublin, particularly in those remote parts of the town. They are of great use to the poor owners, in supplying them with milk—and the young they mostly sell to the masters of ships, who likewise keep them on board their vessels for the sake of their milk.

Labour is generally low, and so are provisions; but those they have mostly within themselves, and of cloaths they require but few. The wife and girls must spin for their own, or want them, so the man has only to provide for his own wants— and a few articles will serve him—
sometimes

sometimes one will suffice—and that is whiskey. This I believe to be the most common way of life—yet it must give place to many (—I heartily wish there were more) exceptions.

Onions are plentiful in Dublin. The Irish seem to be extremely fond of that wholesome root, as well as of potatoes; which is the reason of their being so universally propagated in Ireland.——The constant cry—-"Cheap onions! three pints a penny!" was so often rung in my ears, that whenever I dream of being in Dublin—whatever pursuits my idle fancy may suggest, I am sure of meeting with that salute.—Tripes, with onion-sauce, is a beloved dish at most tables, at least once a week—but particularly on Saturdays.

Walking

Walking one day along the north-side of the river—paffed the barracks—through Phœnix park—croffed the river at Bridge town, a little before I came into the circular-road—in a large field adjacent to the out-fkirts of the town, I faw a man digging:—I went towards him—when I came near to him I perceived he was making a grave.—I began to look about me for a church,—I could fee none—nor any thing like one,—neither a chapel, nor any houfe like a chapel—I then enquired of the honeft man to what church or meeting the burying ground belonged;—he told me, it belonged to no church or meeting in particular. To what fect did it belong?—To any fect. Who then were they who buried there?—The poor.—Did a prieft attend the

K         corps

corps to or at the grave?—Sometimes —those who could afford it had one. —Did any sing before the corps, or at the grave?—No, but they *howled*. —This howling is the ancient manner of lamenting the dead, and is yet retained among the lower people. The howlers are usually hired, especially those who attend the grave at certain hours for some days after the corps has been interred.

There are eight newspapers published in Dublin. The Weekly journal is three halfpence, the other seven are sold at one penny each. The advertisements in most of these papers are printed verbatim from the MSS. and therefore it is no wonder if they are literary curiosities.

Sir, Yours, &c.<br>LETTER

# LETTER X.

## KILKENNY STAGE-COACH.

SIR,

THERE are two Kilkenny stage-coaches; the one sets out from Dublin every Monday, the other every Thursday. The distance between the two places is fifty-six Irish, or seventy-one English, miles, which, in Summer, is travelled in one day; in Winter, in two days. The places I noted in the way were the following:

|  | Irish miles. |
|---|---|
| From Dublin to Rathcool | 7 |
| Thence to Johnstown | 5 |
| ———— Naas | 2 |
| ———— Timolin | 14 |
| ———— Castle-Dermot | 5 |
| ———— Carlow | 6 |
| ———— Leighlin-bridge | 4 |
| ———— Kilkenny | 13 |
| From Dublin to Kilkenny | 56 |

On Thursday, October the 31st, I set out from George-street, in company with a single lady. As soon as we were well awaked, and day-light had broke into our crazy vehicle, a little small-talk prefaced a general conversation, and introduced a better acquaintance. As the lady had

had been but a short time in Dublin, no more than I, both were taken up with alternately relating the most striking incidents we had there met with. The play-house furnished a large store for discussion. America supplied us with much matter—and, both being but lukewarm, our political opinions happily coincided. And thus we agreeably passed the morning, and I thought I was well provided for the day; for the lady, though inclined somewhat to the masculine, was yet of an obliging disposition, and not unentertaining.

About eleven o'clock we came into Johnstown, where we got breakfast -and very acceptable it was, as I well remember to have been extremely hungry;—light wigs,—and fresh

fresh eggs to our tea, with a craving vacuum ready to receive them—not the least invitation was required. We sat down without ceremony, and rose up perfectly satisfied. I was now in raptures with Ireland;—I could not restrain the acclamation---" I was in love with Ireland." This I perceived sounded rather strange in my companion's ears— as she had not before understood me to be a foreigner;---however our friendship was not abated.---We mounted our carriage again, and drove off. We had not gone far when something singular catched my eye---(my companion all the while eying me)—It was a stick, with a white rag at the end of it, stuck in the thatch over the door of a cabin, by the side of the road. I inquired the meaning of it:---The lady,

lady, very obligingly, told me it was the symbol of--" Milk sold here." In turn I was asked a question---" Did I know Mr. Twiss?" But, for the sake of preserving a good understanding between us, I avoided as much as I could entering into any discourse about Mr. Twiss;---yet, I must own, I did not relish very well many of her aspersions, and I soon found I had said enough to awaken her suspicion of my opinion. I am sensible that she now looked on me with no better face than she would have put on to Mr. Twiss himself, had he been in the coach.---How changed the scene!---How vigilant is jealousy!---Nothing escapes it,---Little will produce it,---yet the world itself cannot contain it. It is readily generated from the seeds of interrogation,

gation, and feldom fails of meeting with ample nourifhment even in the moft barren imagination.

A fullen afpect now mantled my lady's cheek——and not a word dropped from her lips;—nor did I once difturb her quiet. She had her humour, and I had mine. A gloomy fleep next clofed her eye-lids—I opened the fafh and looked about me.

The peafants and cottagers, both men and women, were bufy in the fields taking up their potatoes. I more than once counted upwards of a fcore in one field, at that employment.——Some of the women had their children tied on their backs, others were laid on the ground,

ground, at a little diſtance from them, while they followed their work.——The inſtrument they uſe at this work reſembles the common ſpade in England, but its mouth is narrower, and rather longer. When we came near any of them, I always obſerved they left off working———and, reſting their arms upon their ſpades, gazed at us almoſt as far as they could ſee us :——They never indeed appear in a haſte — —they work gently, and I am perſuaded an Engliſh farmer would be but ill pleaſed with their days-works.

A ſudden jolt wakened Mrs. O'——, and I was extremely glad to find her ſhort nap had metamorphoſed her features.—She ſtretched ed herself out————yawned a heigh-ho!————set her hands on her sides, and put on a smile. Her looks told me————" She was sorry if she had given offence————but hoped we would be friends again."————I was not far behind in signifying to her in like manner, that————" If I had said any thing amiss, I humbly asked her pardon."————However this was done without ever a syllable from either side, and we sat without many words for some time, and I believe, would have continued longer so, if another curious sign had not introduced us to each other;————Introduced? you will say,————yes, introduced; for it happened when her good mood was predominant—she turned her best side towards

towards it——she saw it with her naked eye clearly, and not through me darkly. The object was no constellation, though I named it a sign—nor was it indeed a wonder or miracle,——but only these four plain words, on a board, at the side of a cabin-door (—or chimney, which you will)—" Dry Lodgings and tobacco"——(both sold here, I suppose-----). They were profoundly humble lodgings—but whether they were altogether dry, I cannot say.—I noticed many such signs before I came to Kilkenny: Some had—" Good dry Lodgings"—only; others,—" Good dry Lodgings and Snuff."——In the whole road from Dublin to Kilkenny, universal accommodations are to be met with. The best

best inns are fit for the reception of the greatest gentlemen, and the worst cabins will furnish good dry lodgings for the poorest beggar.

I am, Sir,

Yours, &c.

LETTER

## LETTER XII.

*KILKENNY STAGE-COACH,*

*continued.*

SIR,

ABout six o'clock in the evening we came to Timolin, where we dined, supped, and lodged that night. I found nothing here that attracted my notice, nor do I recollect any thing I saw, or any circumstance that happened, worth relating to you.

Between five and six o'clock next morning we set forward on our way to to Kilkenny. We stopt a few minutes at Carlow, which is a pretty neat town, situated on the river Barrow. It is the chief town in the county of the same name. The ale that is brewed here, is reputed to be the best in Ireland: It is pale—very good, and at a penny a pint, the usual price. It is sold in Dublin in bottles. Here are a jail and sessions-house; they are both under one roof, near the middle of the town. Before the front is a court-yard, encompassed by a low wall, and within this space are other prisons, as stocks, a whipping-post, a pillory, and some others I could not make out the particular use of.——Near this town is a quarry of Granite, and, at a little a little diſtance, one of black marble.

Between Carlow and Leighlin-bridge, you have the river Barrow all the way on your right hand; in ſome places it comes cloſe by the ſide of the road, and adds much to the pleaſantneſs of the country, and completes an agreeable proſpect. There are many hills on both ſides, which, by their beautiful verdure appear to be good ſoil, and have great numbers of cattle feeding upon them. This was the fineſt country I ſaw in Ireland;——the land is naturally good, and the labour of the peaſant cannot be overlooked.

We breakfasted at Leighlinbridge. The name of this place is generally pronounced Loughlonbridge, and is sometimes written so. We were shewn into a cold room;——but a servant-girl soon followed us with materials for a fire. She had in either hand a basket. I asked her what she had got there;—" This, sir, said she, ——turning up one of the baskets towards me—is what we call turf ——and this——holding aside the other basket——is what we call wood." The turf was of that kind they call hand turf, which is wrought by hand, or with an instrument resembling a brake, after it is dug out of the earth; and then it is cut into square pieces like bricks; This sort is said to be as good

good as the Dutch turf. The thing she called wood in her other basket was chips.

In going out of Leighlin-bridge we crossed the river Barrow on a plain bridge. The river is now on your left hand, and continues within sight for about half a mile; and then vanishes between two hills.

In many fields the corn was yet standing out, and in others were haycocks. One field of hay I noticed was not all mown.

Two neat gentlemen's seats presented themselves on the right, the one about four, the other six miles from Leighlin-bridge. Within two miles of Kilkenny; on the left, is the

the moſt antique, whimſical building my eyes ever beheld. Sometimes I fancied it to be a church—at other times a fort—at laſt, the number of chimneys convinced me that it was a dwelling-houſe. It covers much ground—is only one ſtory high—has large gothick windows, with ſtone caſes and pillars——is whited on the outſide—and, to crown all——is covered with ſtraw. Who was the architect I know not—but, if I may hazard a conjecture—perhaps it has been *Nimre*, Noah's grandſon, who built Babylon and Ninevah.

On the right, a little before you enter Kilkenny, is a ſmall building, on a hill, called the Gazabo, or Helſham's Folly. It commands an extenſive five profpect, and feems to have been defigned for a Summer or banquetting houfe. It was built by a nephew of the late ingenious Dr. Helfham, who is alfo dead.

I am, Sir,

Yours, &c.

## LETTER XIII.

*KILKENNY.*

SIR,

FROM this road the town of Kilkenny appears to be situated in a valley, and is not seen till you are very near it. The only object that attracts your eye, at the first sight, is the castle, which stands on a rising ground, on the south-side of the town. It consists of two circular buildings, connected by an arch, or large coach-way. The circular parts have conical roofs; and on the top of each is a vane and gilt ball. Some other neat buildings may be distinguished on the slopes, which, on recollecting the common phrase phrafe—" Kilkenny ftreets are paved with marble"—ferve to fill the traveller's head with great expectations—he looks for little lefs than a paradife,—but he finds himfelf wretchedly difappointed on entering the town, where he ftill fees—Good dry lodgings—many times repeated in paffing a long, narrow, dirty, ftreet—built moftly of morter or mud, fods, ftraw, and fuchlike materials. However he is a little brightened when he advances as far as the new bridge, where is a grand opening, decorated with fome neat buildings.

The town is interfected, in two places, by the river Noer; over which are two neat bridges.—Between the river and canal is a pleafant walk ornamented with trees. The canal is not completed, nor perhaps never will,

as

as it has, for some years, been entirely neglected. While they were carrying it on with much spirit, an inundation unfortunately swept away one of the bridges, and, money not being over-plentiful, the cash already subscribed for making the canal was applied to the building of a new bridge.

There is but one parish-church, besides the cathedral, in Kilkenny; and these seem to be sufficient, as the greater part of the inhabitants are Roman-catholics.

On Sunday morning (November 3d) I was desirous of going to church. I was at a private lodging-house, in a very decent family—I respected them much. I enquired if any lodger, or any of the family, were going to church—O yes—many—Miss F—— for one was

was going—very well—she was ready—so much the better:—I soon got ready, and we set forward *tete-a-tete*. After we had gone a little way together, I inquired of my fair companion to which of the churches she was going—she startled—and looked—as if I had frighted her—Nay! was I not going to mass?—p-x on your mass, thought I, and you too! This is the consequence of being led by a woman—I wished myself back, and overhead in bed again a hundred times.—Here we stood—in the public street—each gazed at the other—and both looked like you will easily guess what. After we had recovered a little from our embarrassment, and our features had pretty well reassumed their natural form, I desired the lady to direct me the way to the cathedral—she did, very civilly, so we exchanged a good morning and parted.

The

The cathedral, in the whole, is not beautiful; it has neatnefs, but is deftitute of grandeur. The fervice began at eleven o'clock, and ended at one. The organ is a pretty good one; on the fide of it, in the fame gallery, fix or eight boys were fitting with furplices on—fome of them had neither ftocking nor fhoe on—they fung Sternhold and Hopkins to the Magdalen-chapel tunes. The congregation was remarkably fmall, and, in general, paltry. I noticed fome handicrafts with their aprons tied about them, and others that had them tucked up by a corner.——In returning home, I could not, without fome difficulty, pafs along a part of the High-ftreet, near the Tholfel, for a croud of men and women affembled there, dreffed in their working habits, and each

each with a tool like a fpade. On inquiry, I was told, they were ftanding there to be hired by the Peafants, for the Week, to take up potatoes: And this it feems is the practice every Sunday during the reaping feafon.

Neceffaries, of almoft every kind, are cheap here. Fine wheat-flour was then fold at feven-pence and eight-pence a ftone;——Beef and Mutton at two-pence a pound;— Fowls both wild and tame, are in great plenty, and generally fold at moderate prices; and the Country abounds with Hares.————The horned cattle refemble thofe of Chefhire. The fheep are of a middle fize, and the Mutton is of an exceeding fine flavour. It is common in England to see a pudding within a roast Hare, but here it is quite the reverse; they roast the Hare within a pudding, much in the same manner as we do other Venison.

Near the town are many Coal-pits, and some Marble-quarries. The Coal is of a very extraordinary quality: It produces no smoke, or very little, in burning, but sends out a strong sulphurine vapour, which is often prejudicial, when their funnels do not draw well. But perhaps this may not be wholly an effect of the pernicious matter given out by the Coal, but partly a consequence of the adust air in the room;

room; and I often thought the mouth of their chimnies were but ill-contrived for carrying off the light air and vapours. It is not ſo inflammable as Newcaſtle Coal, but it is more durable. The firſt or morning fire, as they call it, laſts till about two o'clock in the afternoon, when it is made up again, by fixing in freſh coals between the bars, and laying the ſmall on the top, and that without any aſſiſtance or ſtirring, will ſerve till about ten at night. Some have funnels of tin fixed on the tops of their chimneys. Theſe are of two parts, the whole forming a kind of an inverted L, which having a joint in the angle, the upper or horizontal part turns round like a vane, and by that means

means avoids sudden gusts of wind, and more freely emits the vapours, which otherwise might be forced down again. A contrivance of this kind would probably be of good use for curing smoky Houses, and, as it is recommended by Mr. Emmerson, in his Miscellaneous Tracts, I suppose it has been tried, and has answered the purpose, else, I am persuaded, it had never appeared in any Work of that celebrated Author's.——— The Coals are sold in Kilkenny at nine pence or ten-pence a hundred weight, which is nearly equal to four-pence a bushel.

I have read somewhere, that Kilkenny enjoys the four Elements

ments in perfection, which is verfified thus:

Fire without Smoke, and Earth without Bog,
Water without Mud, and Air without Fog.

Ireland abounds in Bogs, Lakes, Rivulets, and Springs, all which together with the beautiful Verdure of the furface, proceed perhaps entirely from the moifture of the Climate, and the Temperature of the Air. But the county of Kilkenny is one of the few that is exempt from Bogs, at leaft they are not fo numerous there as in moft others, and near the town in particular no fuch thing as a real Bog is to be found, which is owing to a ftratum of Gravel and Stones, lying next under a thin covering of Soil on the Surface. And this disposition I likewise take to be at least one cause of the pellucidity of the Water. But I had all along, from my first setting foot in the island, observed, That the Waters issuing from the Springs were generally not so clear as the Spring-water is commonly seen in England; and therefore, this like the former, being a rare Phenomenon in Ireland, has been particularly remarked, and far too universally understood.

I was assured positively, That in and about Kilkenny they never have any Fogs. Yet, I do not at all doubt, but that, in every

every Season of the Year, especially in Winter, the clouds are at different heights, from different Causes; but then I understand, they are never discovered to be so low as in many other places, nor to be connected with any visible exhalations ascending from the surface of the Earth. If this be true, as I believe it is, the quality of the exhalations, and the situation of the place, will be the principal, if not the only Causes. The narrow Vale along which the river runs, opening wide just by the side of the town, must contribute much to the clearing away of moist Vapours, and to rendering the Air more pure and wholesome.

The

The Marble which is in great plenty here is black ſtreaked with white. It bears an exceeding fine Poliſh, and is the common material for chimney pieces. The Pillars (inſtead of Poſts which guard the ſide, or foot, Walks, in the Streets, are of Marble; and, for ought I know the Stones in the pavements are rough Marble. The ſtreets are generally well paved, but are poſſeſt of no peculiar elegance that I could ſee. Moſt of the common (or cobble) ſtones or thoſe dug out of the Earth for common uſe, are either a ſpecies of, or nearly reſemble, Marble. Out of a ſtone-wall, which ſeparates in one place the River and Canal, I numbered at random ſeveral parcels

cels of ſtones, and found the proportion of thoſe of Marble to thoſe of other ſorts, as thirteen to one.

I am, dear Sir,

Yours, &c.

LETTER

## LETTER XIV.

*A Description of the CAVERNS near KILKENNY.*

SIR,

AT a little distance from the town are a number of caverns, which, by the inhabitants, are esteemed the greatest curiosities of the kind in the world. But whether they who gave me this information of them had either seen or read of those at Antiparos, and some others, I know not—— I suppose they never had. They are

are near the Park-houfe of Donmore, and are defcribed by an ingenious Gentleman, who lately vifited them, in the following words:

"After a difficult defcent of about one hundred feet, the entrance into this fubterraneous world is gained. The appearance of the firft Cavern is uncommonly awful, and gives rife to an idea of a grand Gothick Structure in ruins. The folemnity of this place is not a little encreafed by the gaiety of thofe fcenes which prefent themfelves on every fide, previous to our entering it. The floor is uneven, and ftones of various fizes are promifcuoufly difperfed upon it. The fides are compofed of ragged

ged work in some places covered with moss, and in others curiously frosted; and from the roof, which is a kind of arch, several huge rocks project beyond each other in such a manner that they seem to threaten instant ruin.

The circumference of this Cave is not less than two hundred feet, and its height above fifty. Here is a small but continually dropping water from the cieling, and a few petrefactions resembling isicles. This place is not destitute of inhabitants; for immediately on entering into into it you are surprized with a confused noise, which is occasioned by a multitude of wild pigeons. Hence there is a passage towards the left, where, by a small ascent, a kind of hole is gained, much larger, but in form greatly resem-

resembling the mouth of an oven, which introduces the spectator to a place, where, by the help of candles, (day-light being entirely excluded) a broken and surprizing scene of monstrous stones heaped on each other, chequered with various colours, inequality of rocks overhead, and an infinity of stalactical stones, presents itself. Nature, one would imagine, designed the first Cave as a preparative for what remains to be seen; by it the eye is familiarized to uncommon and awful objects, and the mind tolerably fortified against those ideas which result from a combination of appearances, unthought of, surprizing and menacing. The spectator flatters himself that he has nothing to behold more awful, nor any thing

thing more dangerous to meet, than what he finds in the firſt cavern—but he ſoon diſcovers his miſtake; for the bare want of that light which dreſſes nature with gaiety, is alone ſufficient to render the ſecond far more dreadful. In the firſt he fancies ruin frowns upon him from ſeveral Parts; but in this it is threatened from a thouſand vaſt rocks rudely piled on each other, that compoſe the ſides, which ſeem bending in; and a multitude, of no ſmaller ſize, are pendant from the Roof, in the moſt extraordinary manner: Add to this, that, by one falſe ſtep, he would be daſhed from precipice to precipice. Indeed it would be a Matter of much difficulty, or rather impracticable, to walk over this apartment, had not nature,

nature, as if studious for the safety of the curious, caused Branches, as it were, to shoot from the surface of the rocks, which are remarkably smooth, very unequal, and always damp. These branches are from four to six inches in length, and nearly as thick. They are useful on the summits of the rocks to prevent slipping, and in the sides are ladders, whereby to descend and ascend with tolerable facility. This astonishing amfractuous passage leads to a place far more curious than the rest. On entering into it, one is almost induced to believe oneself situated in an ancient temple, decorated with all the expence of art; yet, notwithstanding the beauty and splendor that catches the eye on every side, there is something

thing of solemnity in the fashion of the place, which must be felt by the most inattentive spectator. The floor, in some parts, is covered with a crystalline substance; the sides, in many places, are incrusted with the same, wrought in a taste not unlike the Gothick style of ornament, and the top is almost entirely covered with inverted pyramids of the same elegantly white and lucid matter. At the points of these stalactical streets are perpetually hanging drops of pellucid water, for when one falls another succeeds. These pendant gems contribute not a little to the glory of the roof, which, when the place is properly illuminated, appears as if formed of the purest crystal. Here are three extraordinary and beautiful congelations,

tions, which, without the affiftance of a ftrong imagination, may be taken for an organ, altar, and crofs. The former, except when ftrictly examined, appears to be a regular work of art, and is of a confiderable fize; the fecond is of a fimple form, rather long than fquare; and the third reaches from the floor to the roof, which muft be about twenty feet. Thefe curious figures are owing to water that falls from the upper parts of the cave to the ground, which coagulated into ftone from time to time, till it acquired thofe forms which are now fo pleafing; or to an exfudation or extillation of petrefying juices out of the earth; or perhaps they partake of the nature of fpar, which is a kind of rock-plant.

The former seems the most probable supposition, as these figures, in colour and consistence, appear exactly like the isicles on the top, which are only seen from the wet parts of the caverns; and, in this place, there is a greater oozing of water, and a much larger number of petrefactions, than in any other. When you quit this curious apartment, the guides lead you for a considerable way through winding places, until a glimmering light agreeably surprizes. Here the journey, of above a quarter of a mile, through those parts is ended: But, upon returning into the first cavern, the entrance into other apartments, less curious indeed, but as extensive as those we have described, offers itself. The passages into

into some of these are so very low, that there is a necessity of creeping through them; by these we proceed until the noise of a subterraneous river is heard, but farther none have ventured."

Sir,

Yours, &c.

LETTER

## LETTER XV.

*Further Remarks and Occurrences in the County of KILKENNY.*

SIR,

THIS County supplies Dublin with a great quantity of wheat, or rather wheat-flour, which is packed up in sacks, and conveyed on cars.———Walking one Day by the side of the river, near some corn-mills, I was met by a flour-car; the driver, who was seated on the thill, was a mean-looking, ragged youth. Just as I had passed him, he accidently dropped

ped his rod out of his hand; when another youth, of nearly the same complexion with himself, coming along the Road, readily stepped aside, took up the rod, and, very politely, presented it to its owner. This occasioned many compliments. Monsieur himself could not have made a better leg than the presenter. Each waved his hat——— bowed————recovered————turned ——— then parted, and covered. ————Instances of this sort may be observed hourly in the streets of Kilkenny; which shew that they are before-hand with their neighbours, the English, in the fine art of politeness, how far soever they may fall behind in other arts and sciences.

Learning,

Learning, I believe, is much neglected in most parts of Ireland; at least it is not pursued with so much ardor as in England. There are indeed some good schools in the island, and it is well known they have sent out scholars that yield not the palm to any in Europe. At Kilkenny is a flourishing school, established upon a Plan similar to that at Westminster. Many distinguished persons now living received the rudiments of their education at this school. One of the best orators perhaps in the British parliament was educated here.———And it was here I was first informed of the Longitude being found out in Ireland;—that the gentleman who had discovered (or rather compleated) it, resided mostly, and was then in in Dublin————that he wrote to Lord Sandwich about a year ago, informing him of the important invention, and had received an anſwer, requeſting his attendance at the board of Longitude in London, at the next meeting——but that he refuſed to comply with the propoſal, on account of no, or at leaſt inadequate, premium offered him in hand. The method of performing this great work was hit upon many years ago by a gentleman in Dublin,—he purſued it with ſingular application, till remorſeleſs Time diſqualified him for the celeſtial taſk;————Death ſoon after cloſed the ſcene—and the common terreſtrial portion was his lot at laſt. But fortunately his labours were not buried with him. The

The whole affair was communicated to a friend—the gentleman now poſſeſſed of the ſecret, who has, by a like aſſiduity, completed the work——the principal deſideratum in the whole circle of human learning. But I am much afraid that this, like many other attempts which have vaniſhed long before it, will at laſt prove but a phantom: For it is a lamentable truth—that in matters of ſo important and difficult a nature, men are often puſhed forward, and even blinded, by a kind of preſumptive and ſelf-conceited zeal, which demonſtration itſelf can hardly ſtop the career of. And, in the caſe before us, one would think that the premiums propoſed in the act were alone ſufficient, without any other proviſion, to incite

incite solid merit to unfold its contents. Rational truth will not seek for more, and it is sure of meeting with no less. But the vain imaginer is terrified with the very thoughts of an open examination—he then finds a doubt where before he looked for no such thing—and his chimerical fabrick is shaken to the very foundation, even in his own breast, before it is assailed, But I do not say, that this of which I am speaking is a chimera; nor do I positively affirm it is not——I only hope it is not. The author, who is in great reputation in Dublin for his learning, seems to be thoroughly convinced of its truth and utility; and if it proves so easy and practicable as he announces it to be, his name will be remembered and revered as long as the world endures.

I have now nothing more to add from this quarter. But as you may reasonably suppose that I have heard something about these seditious people commonly known by the name of *Whiteboys*, who infest this and some of the neighbouring counties, I will therefore give you an account of them, from Mr. Twifs's Tour, which I always found to correspond with the results of my own inquiries about them.

" The Counties of Kilkenny, Waterford, Wexford and Carlow, are over-run with ruffians called Whiteboys. These are peasants, who do not choose to pay tythes

or

or taxes, and who in the nighttime affemble, fometime to the number of many hundreds, on horseback, and on foot, well armed, and with fhirts over their cloaths, from whence their denomination is derived, when they ftroll about the country, firing houfes and barns, burying people alive in the ground, cutting their nofes and ears off, and committing other barbarities on their perfons. The objects of their revenge and cruelty are chiefly tythe and tax gatherers, and landlords who attempt to raife their rents; they never rob; neither do they moleft travellers. Rewards of forty and fifty pounds are continually advertifed in the papers for apprehending any one of them; and from time to time a few of thefe

*deluded*

*deluded* Wretches (as the advertisements term them) are hanged, and escorted to the gallows by a regiment of soldiers. Excommunications are likewise read against them by their priests from the pulpit; but as they are so numerous it is not likely that they will be soon extirpated."——He adds further—" A few years ago, a like set of insurgents, who wore oak-leaves in their hats, and called themselves *Oakboys*, rose in the North of Ireland. Those gentry refused paying the tythe of their potatoes, telling their priests that they ought to be satisfied with their tythe of what grew above ground. The disturbances which they caused are now at an end; as I was informed that they carried their point by being so numerous,

merous, and that at present their potatoes are tythe-free."

On Monday, November 4th, I left Kilkenny, and reached Dublin the evening of the next Day.

Sir,

Your, &c.

## LETTER XIV.

*Miscellaneous Observations———on the peculiar CUSTOMS, &c. of the IRISH.*

SIR,

I Will now close my account of Ireland with informing you of such singular customs of the people, as came to my knowledge from the people themselves, without paying any regard to what others have, or might have, written on the subjects.

I. The

I. The extravagant and univerſal uſe of potatoes is ſo well known, that I might very well paſs it over without ever a word, and without much impropriety; but as I was ſo often ſerved with them, in their native hue, and in ſuch huge quantities, which far exceeded all that I had ſuggeſted from previous intelligence, you muſt permit me to add a little to the current Account. Theſe are always ſerved up unpeeled——each Perſon at the table peeling his own, if he chooſes them ſo,——but ſome do not take that trouble, but only cut them into Quarters, and lay them by the ſides of their plates in the place of bread. The ladies (——to be ſure!——) always peel their

potatoes

potatoes———and, moſt politely, depoſite them (ſmoaking hot) on the cloth, by their plates. The firſt time I was treated in this manner, I confeſs I could hardly keep my temper———daubing one's fingers———ſeeing the Table ſtrewed all over with peelings ———which often catch you by the arm or hand———In ſhort, I looked upon myſelf as a partner in a ſcene of genuine ſluttery. But a little further experience taught me to expect no better: The diſappointment indeed was ſoon taken off, but the diſagreeableneſs ſtill remained the ſame. There is nothing to be met in the whole iſland, I will venture to affirm, in which an Engliſhman cuts ſo bad a figure, as in this of *peeling his*

*his potatoes.* If he be an entire ſtranger in the country, and not of a very cool, harmleſs nature——— he is certainly difguſted while he has his potatoe on his fork ;——— but if he is inclined in the leaſt to a wag———ten to one but he burſts out into open laughter during the operation.———The apology made for this filthy cuſtom, which they very know is not agreeable to moſt foreigners, is extremely delicate and convincing— They tell you, that they do not think it proper to let their potatoes go through the fervants' dirty fingers ; and befides, by keeping them in the peeling, they retain their heat longer.

II. Boiled

II. Boiled eggs to tea in the morning, is a custom almost as universal as potatoes at dinner——— and to this I give my most cordial approbation. An egg or two, or sometimes three or four, are eaten to toast, or bread and butter, or saffron wigs; after which they drink their tea. They seem to be exceedingly careful (and they are in the right) in choosing their eggs fresh.——— Eggs are very plentiful in Ireland, even in Dublin. In some places, in the spring, they are so cheap as ten or twelve a penny.

III. I never saw but one pudding while I was in the country. They censure, and even affect to deride the English for restraining flesh from their children, and feeding them

them with pudding. I do not know whether this language is agreeable to the doctrine of their phyficians———but I believe it will concord with the general opinion of the people. They hold it facred to keep their children to their athletic ftate,——— and to be fure they have fenfe enough to love themfelves. What avails felf-denial———or pale faced temperance?———Nothing but to reduce a man (an Irifhman) to a child ———to an afs———to worfe, to a fkeleton.———Avaunt, fuch ghaftly fpectres!———fuch meagre deities!———Give Hibernia's fons plenty——— a folid round of beef, and a big-bellied bottle———thefe are the gods for them! But, ferioufly, as long as this way of thinking

ing prevails in Ireland, or indeed in any other country, that country in my Opinion never will make any figure in the more substantial and serious part of the world.

IV. The peasants' houses are, in general, but little better than the cabins. The difference consists in the former having a chimney, or a hole in the roof———a window of about a foot square, in the front, and a whited outside, in imitation of their tyrannic lord's. And this custom of whiting the outsides of their houses, to me seems to be well suited to the fine verdure so peculiarly distinguished in this island. But, better would it be for those poor, laborious, and, permit me to say, *honourable*, set of people; and
the

## KILKENNY.

the country in general, were the infides of their huts more ferioufly attended to:——Hunger and ftarvation are too often to be found within. The Polifh peafants, I verily believe, live better, and are more looked upon, than thofe neglected, miferable beings. The primary caufe of this wretchednefs lies in the owners of the lands—— in their not refiding in the country, who therefore find it more agreeable to let out their eftates in large parcels or farms to other gentlemen of lefs fortune, who are thence ufually diftinguifhed by the appellation of *Leafe-holders*. Thefe gentlemen (——terrible gentlemen!) let out the lands in fmall farms, to poor tenants, who are, by contract, obliged to build their own houfes, houses, and fit up such other conveniences as they find wanting and necessary. But these conveniences are only temporary—— contrived to endure just the length of their term, and no longer; and by this means each succeeding tenant enters on the premises as his predecessor did before him.————— After this narration, I will not presume to draw you out of the evident inferences———— the consequence of the want of food, it is plain, is real hunger, and that of cloths is literal starvation——— but let these suffice———— the reflection is painful to me. One thing, however, I cannot forbear to lament————— That those non-residents are not taxed. It has been agitated, I know,

know, and I hope it will go forward. That would be ſtriking at the very root of many diſorders and calamities now raging amongſt them, and would conduce much to improvements of every kind.

V. There is a very rude, and not leſs extraordinary uſage, yet practiſed in Ireland, which, one might ſuppoſe would ſeem too prepoſterous even to a Muſſulman in this age of the World. It is this——When a Man is in love with a Woman, but is repulſed by her relations, he often has recourſe to the following ſtratagem:— He cauſes a report to be ſpread in the neighbourhood, that he intends to carry her off

(—not

(———not to Gretna-green——— but to where he pleases—). This seldom fails of gaining the point. He is now permitted to pay his addresses without interruption, and is generally looked on by the whole family as a true and sincere lover. When this is the case, matters are soon settled, and all ends in peace and unity: But if he falls short by this menace, a set of ruffians are employed to execute the wicked project, who watch an opportunity of laying hold of the young woman———she is forcibly carried off, she knows not whither and the brutal usage afterwards met with, she perhaps never returns to relate.—I knew not of any such custom till I came into Dublin,

Dublin, nor did I pay much regard to the story, till I became acquainted with one who unfortunately knew it too well.

VI. Of all the peculiarities to be found in Ireland, the moſt ſurprizing is that of the country being freed from venomous animals of every kind. The truth of this exemption has been queſtioned, and by ſome flatly denied; but it is a fact beyond all doubt. The reaſon remains yet a ſecret; it has hitherto fallen without the reach of all the writers who have mentioned it——— and it has yet eluded all my beſt endeavours, though I ſtill retain ſome hope, that, with a few hints from any gentleman acquainted with moſt parts of the iſland, and who has

has turned his thoughts that way, the matter may be expounded, and the whole perhaps clearly accounted for.

There are five packets which fail between Dublin and Holyhead. This is the commoneſt track from Dublin to London, as well as to moſt other places in England, and I believe it is one of the ſafeſt; but to or from the ſouthmoſt counties, the beſt way is in one of the yachts which ſail between Milford and Waterford;——and from any part of Scotland, or the county of Northumberland, the Donaghadee and Portpatrick Sloop will be moſt convenient, as well as the ſpeedieſt and ſafeſt paſſage,——the time on the ſea, at this place, is ſeldom more

more than three hours, and I could not hear of one single misfortune that had ever happened to any passenger.

On the tenth of November I embarked in the Besborough packet, and in ten or eleven hours arrived safe at Holyhead.

Sir,

Yours, affectionately.

LETTER

## LETTER XVII.

*WALES,——viz. The Island of Anglesey,—Carnarvonshire,—Denbighshire,—Flintshire,—to Chester.*

SIR,

AT Holyhead are two genteel Inns, at either of which a stage-coach is always ready to take up Passengers from the packets. In these coaches you are conveyed to Chester in two days, and for thirty shillings;—— the distance is ninety-three miles. From Chester you have to make out your own particular road, and are at liberty to choose

choose your carriage, or any other mode of travelling. This Island (Anglesey) is twenty-five miles over, measured along the road from Holyhead to Bangor Ferry. The other particular places and distances I remarked were the following:

|  | Miles. |
|---|---|
| From Holyhead to Bangor Ferry | 25 |
| Thence to Bangor — | 2 |
| ———— Penmaen Maur | 11 |
| ———— Conway — | 8 |
| ———— Burtree-hill | 3 |
| ———— Penmaen Rofs | 5 |
| ———— Abergely — | 4 |
| ———— Rilland Marsh | 2 |
| ———— St. Asaph — | 5 |
| ———— Holywell — | 10 |
| ———— Chester — | 18 |
| From Holyhead to Chester | 93 |

On

On coming to the Inn, in Holyhead, on Sunday night, whither we were conducted by the Boatmen who set us ashore, we were saluted by music and dancing. As I could not make out what kind of an instrument it could be, having never heard such music before, I intimated a desire of being introduced into the room, but, on being informed by the Waiter, that it was a select company of gentlemen and ladies, who had come in the stage that day, and were intending to proceed in the packet to Dublin the next day, I returned to my own companions, and took no further thought about them. The instrument, I was told, was a Welsh Harp; an instrument peculiar to the country, and agreeable enough to the ear.
—Next

——Next morning, after breakfast, we proceeded on our journey. We had not got far before we were met by three of Sir John Fielding's Men,——and on inquiry it appeared, that they were pursuing those very gentry who, the night before, had been so exceedingly happy.—— ~~Good God~~!——of what a texture are the minds of some people!——Composed and easy in the very lap of wickedness.——Where was conscience?——Conscience had not been within.——But alas!—if he had—what could he have done, when superannuated—feeble—forlorn—nay, in all probability, turned quite out of doors?——Alas, poor conscience!——When this is the case—when that fine perception, planted ed by the wife author of our nature, is loft,———when religion morality, and calm reafon, are not permitted to fit in the judgment-feat of the heart, that is, when confcience is not allowed to reign in full majefty,———then is the little republic completely overturned, and the man is loft to all focicty, as well as to himfelf—perhaps for ever———and for ever ———.

In travelling over this ifland, nothing material prefented itfelf. The only thing I noticed was on our right-hand, four or five miles from Holyhead. The tide was flowing, and the wind at fouth-weft. The breakers ftriking with great force againft the large rocks, flew high up in the air, fo that the whole fhore shore appeared as if decked with foaming pyramids of the restless Ocean. But to understand this the better, we must consider, That, at most places on the English side of the channel, the tides rise very rapidly, and very high—to a much greater height than they do on the Irish side. For instance, at Holyhead the tide flows nearly twenty feet, at Conway, in Denbighshire, it flows eighteen feet: but on the opposite side it seldom rises more ten feet in any harbour. And therefore when the tide is flowing, and the wind blows on the land, the percussion against the rocks is then great, and the resistance being equal to it, that is, equal to the momentum of the wave, the water is thereby dashed violently into the air, and the spray appears in such variety of shapes and colours, that the scene is very entertaining and beautiful.

The island, as far as I could view it, seems to be of a remarkably dusky complexion. There are numbers of barren, rocky, mountains, always in sight from the road, and sometimes marshes. But it is already well known, and I can add but little to the descriptions, or to your entertainment.

We came to the Boathouse, which is on the Anglesey side, in little more than five hours. The annual rent of the privilege of this boat, is four hundred pounds. Whence we may conclude, as each passenger pays one shilling, and allowing fifty ty pounds for the subsistence of the tenant, and the number of people who pass and repass this way every year is about nine thousand.—— After ferrying over, another carriage was ready for our reception at the Inn on the other side, which conveyed us to Conway, where we took up our lodgings. The new road along Penmaen Maur was then completed, and is every way much preferable to the old road. It cost two thousand pounds, and was made in pursuance of an act which was obtained in the year 1769.

The next morning, pretty early, we proceeded on our journey.— From Burtree-hill is an extensive prospect; but the Air was so excessively cold on it, that I could find but little pleasure in looking about me.

Penmaen Ross is a mountain consisting of one entire rock.

Just after rising up a hill, from the pleasant village of Abergely, Rilland Marsh appeared on the left hand. It is about four miles from East to West, and upwards of two from the Sea to the foot of the Hill along which we were passing. It is very even, and the eye takes in the whole at one view.

St. Asaph is a very pleasant situation, on a fine plain; there is a small river, over which is a plain bridge of five arches.

Between

Between St. Asaph and Holywell are many Lead-mines on both sides of the road.

Holywell consists of three principal streets, which branch out from the market-place, as from a center. We entered the town at the West street;——turned a little to the right out of the market-place into the South-west street——leaving the North-street on our left hand. At the foot, or extreme, of the North street, is the celebrated Spring known by the name of St. *Winefred's Well.* As this is the place where dinner is commonly provided for the passengers, I employed a few leisure minutes in visiting the Well. I had no need of making much inquiry for the road to it-----there are

are generally people ſtanding ready about the Inn to guide you in the way, if you are a ſtranger and have no idea of its ſituation;-----but theſe Conductors are not eaſily ſatisfied for their trouble though the labour might be abridged to ten words, and a ſlight motion with the right hand;------ but that is a ſpecies of wit incompatible with avarice-----the means would ſubvert the ends. Avarice is always officious, and profuſely laviſh in words and little complimental actions,---theſe are its peculiar characteriſtics----and by theſe it is always known, and eaſily detected.------But to return,------- many attendants are likewiſe conſtantly ſtationed at the Well —— One with a beaker glaſs preſents

sents you with a draught of the water.——Another expatiates on its virtues———gives you a long detail of the many wonderful Cures performed by the use of it, and concludes with a catalogue of the annual and casual Visitants who come thither to bathe, and drink the water,—— and, in this account, you are sure of hearing the names of Dr. Solander and Mr. Banks perhaps more than once mentioned. A third person has papers explaining the origin, &c. of the Spring, and these they sell at sixpence (if possible) or three-pence (if you please.)—The following account is the substance of one of those descriptive papers which are sold at the place.

" The

" The rife of St. Winefred's well is by fome accounted a miracle, and related as follows :——That in the year 700 lived *Winefred*, a virgin of extraordinary fanctity, who made a vow of chaftity during life, and dedicated herfelf to the fervice of God.—A Heathen prince named *Cradoc*, having often attempted Winefred's chaftity in vain, met her fome time after upon the top of the hill near Holywell church, and ftruck off her head, which, rolling down the hill, was taken up by the prieft of Holywell, who being a favourite of the Almighty's, did by divine affiftance, replace the head on Winefred's fhoulders, who was thereby reftored to life, and lived fifteen years afterwards.—— the prefent loofe and degenerate age,

many

many may reckon this relation fabulous; but, if it be confidered, that the Old and New Teftaments furnifh us with many furprizing and miraculous things, done by the power of God and Chrift, there can be no difpute at leaft as to the poffibility of it.——That, at the very inftant Winefred was reftored to life, this Spring arofe, in that very place, no doubt in order to perpetuate the memory of fo great a miracle, which caufed the chriftian religion to increafe in a very extraordinary manner, and Winefred being made a faint, the holy prieft of Holywell named the Spring *St. Winefred's Well*; and indeed the waters feem to be of a fingular nature, and not to be excelled; for, from the original rife of this Spring

to

to this day, the water, by bathing therein, performs wonderful cures:—It heals thofe troubled with the Leprofy, and many other difeafes; reftores the lame to the ufe of their limbs, as well as the blind to their fight, and ftrengthens fuch as are recovered of the fmall-pox. The phyficians are of opinion the water is of that excellent nature as not to be equalled in the univerfe; which has caufed fo great refort, that, from a few houfes, Holywell is increafed to a large Market-town of fine buildings, fufficient to entertain the greateft number of people, and the bathing is every way rendered as agreeable as at any other Wells or Baths.

" Here

"　Here it may not be improper to take notice of what to some people may seem incredible, but the truth of what is offered will at any time be demonstrated to the curious; that is, that by the gauge the Bason and Well hold about two hundred and forty tons of water, which, when let out, fill again in less than two minutes. The experiment was tried for a wager, on Tuesday the 12th of July, 1731; Mr. Price, the rector of Holywell, Mr. Williams, Mr. Wynne, Dr. Taylor, and many other gentlemen of Holywell, as well as strangers, and the writer of this relation, being present; when, to the surprize of the company, the Well and Bason filled in less than two minutes; which plainly shews that this spring raises

raises more than *one hundred tuns* of water every minute. And although the water in the bason is more than four feet deep, it is so transparent that a small piece of money, or a pin, may be seen at the bottom. The water rises up in the Well as if it were in a Brewer's boiler and violently agitated by heat.

" In the bottom of the bason are several large pebble stones, which, to the eye, appear as if besprinkled or besmeared with blood; one of these stones has sometimes the resemblance of a flower-pot when bedecked with the choicest flowers.

" The Water issuing from the Well turns three Mill a-breast, in View,

# KILKENNY. 179

view, and several other mills below them never want water.

We attained Chester before seven o'clock, and the next morning proceeded to Manchester;—the next day we attained Leeds,—the following day Boroughbridge, and the next following, being the sixteenth of November, we arrived in Durham.

I am, dear Uncle,

Yours, &c.

R        M. E.

THE END.

www.ingramcontent.com/pod-product-compliance
Lightning Source LLC
Chambersburg PA
CBHW020243170426
43202CB00008B/205